PRACTICAL FERMENTATION

A WORKING GUIDE TO FERMENTATION KITS

YI ZHANG

CONTENTS

Why Have I Written This Working Guide? 4

1. Why Do We Need Fermented Foods?
1.1 Fermentation is Culture. 7
1.2 Fermented Foods are Gourmet 8
1.3 Fermented Foods are Medicinal 9
1.4 Making Fermented Foods is Self-Sustaining 12

2. How to Use Fermentation Kits
2.1 Introduction to Fermentation Kits. 15
2.2 How to Use Fermentation Kits. 18
2.3 What Else Do I Need? 18
2.4 How Do I Know the Fermentation is Successful? 20
2.5 Storing Your Fermented Products 21

3. Recipes
3.1 Vegetables 23
    Sauerkraut 24
    Kimchi 26
    Ginger carrots. 28
    Pickled radish 30
    Pickled cucumbers 32
    Salsa. 34
    Ketchup 36
    Mom's Sichuan Pao Cai. 38
3.2 Fruits 40
    Pineapple chutney. 40
    Apricot butter. 42
3.3 Beverages 44
    Ginger ale 44
    Beet kvass 45
3.4 Dairy 46
    Kefir 46
    Whey 47
3.5 Grain 48
    Jiu Niang (sweet rice wine). 48
3.6. Making Wine from Fruits 50

WHY HAVE I WRITTEN THIS WORKING GUIDE?

Many people love fermented foods, such as sauerkraut, kimchi and kefir. I am one of them. Making them is a part of my weekly routine. I learned to make fermented foods from my mom, books and through practice.

MY MOM LIKES SICHUAN *PAO CAI*, a kind of traditional fermented vegetable favored by the south-western Chinese. She made it every year and shared it with neighbors and friends. A small bowl of *Pao Cai* was like a loving ambassador, delivering happiness and the delicious flavors to her friends. Sometimes they simply dropped off their jars and vegetables and asked my mom to make more for them. When the *Pao Cai* was done, they came to pick it up! Now mom is in her seventies, but she still makes *Pao Cai* every year. This has been a part of her routine since forever. Her kitchen cannot be without a jar of *Pao Cai*. I believe my mom planted the seed of making fermented foods in my heart.

I used to be a healthcare practitioner and a research scientist. But after more than 10 years of stressful work, I developed rheumatoid arthritis (RA), an autoimmune disorder. Chronic fatigue and joint pain bothered me. I could not prevent myself from getting sick, even though I worked in healthcare! It was frustrating and upsetting. I started to look for solutions other than pharmaceutical pills, because I knew they couldn't get to the root cause of my condition.

The book *Nourishing Traditions*, written by Sally Fallon, changed my view of food. I realized that real food, which is food found in nature without processing, alteration and chemicals, is part of the foundations of good health – and might be a cure for my RA. Seven years ago, not only did I throw away all my processed foods and chose *real*, organic food instead, but I also started to make fermented vegetables and fruits. Those natural and complicated flavors with some sourness and a little sweetness were interesting to me. Then I started to like them and made more and more. I made sauerkraut, dilly beans, apricot butter, kombucha, sourdough bread, kefir… I tried all kinds of interesting recipes. All of these delicious and nutritious fermented foods, combined with other real foods, brought wonderful meals to my family's dining table.

Fermented foods have become a necessary part of my daily meals. Making fermented foods is now my kitchen routine. I realized that fermented foods, together with other lifestyle changes such as exercise, making sure to eat real foods, good sleeping and minimizing the use of electronic devices, are all part of my healing plan. My RA has much improved. Now I am a farmer and gardener, focusing on providing real foods for my family, neighbors and community.

Initially when making fermented foods, I had both successes and failures. My first batch of fermented foods, dilly beans, turned out to be one of my family's favorites. Sometimes, however, I had to discard the whole batch. It takes practice to learn and understand the science, art, benefits and creation behind fermentation.

When I tried fermentation kits, I found they made the process much easier and saved me some effort. However, learning to use them didn't come without some failures, so I was motivated to write this workbook to share some of my experiences with beginners or anyone struggling to perfect fermentation.

To be practical, this book explains why we need fermented foods, how to use fermentation kits, and contains some recipes. I have also included a recipe for no-fuss wine from fruit. There are 16 recipes in this book, and this is because each chef has his or her own creativeness. Once you have understood the basic rules of fermentation, you will be able to adjust the amount of ingredients or to add new ones to develop your favorite flavors. For example, you could take the Pickled Radish recipe (see page 30) and use it to make pickled cauliflower or turnip; or use dried apple, peach or fig to substitute the apricot in the Apricot Butter recipe (see page 42). Just choose one or two recipes which you are interested in and repeat them several times to grasp the skill, and then create your own unique recipes. Enjoy the fun of your creation!

CHAPTER 1

WHY DO WE NEED FERMENTED FOODS?

1.1 Fermentation is Culture.

THE HISTORY OF MAKING fermented food dates back 4,000–5,000 years ago, perhaps even earlier. In the era of Noah, people already knew how to make grape wine, which was recorded in Bible. In ancient China, people brewed beverages from rice and millet, flavored with herbs, flowers, and tree resins (*Fermented beverages of pre-and proto-historic China*. The National Academy of Sciences, 2004). Each regional area has its own special fermented food. For example, kimchi, miso, natto, and tempeh are from Asia. In Africa, they make injera, togwa, and garri. In European countries, kefir, sauerkraut, crème fraiche, and kvass are typical fermented foods. From vegetables, fruits, grains, legumes, and dairy, to fish and meat, people make all kinds of fermented foods.

Why do people do it? Fermentation is culture. It is how people interact with their environment, such as climate, soil, plants, and water, in order to preserve their foods. It develops tradition. People in Korea make kimchi (see page 26), a part of the tradition of Korean cuisine. Korea is located in the Korean Peninsula with hills, mountains, and coastline. Summer is short and humid, and rainfall is heavy. Winters are usually long, cold, and dry. Rice, nappa cabbage, radishes, perrila, Asian pears and apples are their typical produce. In the harvest season, Koreans prepare kimchi and other pickled vegetables for a long and cold winter. This is what they have learned from nature: how to survive in harsh weather using the food they can grow and collect.

Sauerkraut (see page 24) is similar but different from kimchi. This fermented cabbage originates from Germany where it has been a staple in the German diet since the 1600s. In general, Germany's climate is temperate with cold, cloudy winters and warm summers. Oats, berries, milk, cheese, and pork are often used in their meals. White and green cabbages are their typical seasonal vegetables. They can be kept in the field for a long time, and are easy to make into sauerkraut. Roasted pork served with sauerkraut is a standard in German cuisine.

Culture is also the interaction between bacteria and their ecosystem. Lactic acid bacteria, the most well-studied bacteria that creates fermentation, can feed on all kinds of vegetables, fruits, grains and meat; they decompose the nutrients, assemble their own DNA, and then produce and release lactic acid, carbon dioxide, acetic acid, enzymes and vitamins into the environment.

In general, there are two types of fermentation: aerobic and anaerobic. The former needs oxygen and the latter can occur without oxygen. Bacteria, fungi, and their produce, such as enzymes, work together to complete the whole fermentation process: aerobic, anaerobic or both. In the bacteria group, two well-known ones are lactic acid bacteria (LAB) which is anaerobic, and acetic acid bacteria (AAB) which is aerobic. LAB works on vegetables, fruits and dairy, but AAB makes vinegar and kombucha. For fungi, there are aerobic and anaerobic ones too, including yeasts, molds, and mushrooms. Fungi can be used to make bread, miso, beer, and wine. What we need to do is to create and maintain the environment, using temperature, humidity and oxygen, to allow a certain group of bacteria and / or fungi to grow and develop into the finished products that we want.

1.2 Fermented Foods are Gourmet.

Fermented foods have a delicious taste and texture. They have been elaborately prepared by microbial "chefs". Billions of them work together pre-digesting foods, consuming sugars, cutting large starch and protein molecules into small ones. They form their own constituents including lactic acid, amino acids, small molecules of sugar, vitamins, and enzymes. This work not only pre-digests the foods but also adds fragrance, aroma, and improved flavor to them. They satisfy your palate immediately.

Fermented foods go beautifully with all kinds of meat and dairy products. Think about assembling the Reuben sandwich by layering corned beef, cheese, sauerkraut, and sliced tomato. Then serve with a simple green salad. This humble sandwich is delicious any time of year.

Ketchup was originally a fermented food. Now it has become a popular condiment in North America, but it's not fermented. Store-bought ketchup is full of sugar and chemical preservatives, and doesn't contain any beneficial bacteria. Next time, why not make your own home-made fermented ketchup? It's flavorful and rich, and without any additives (see page 36). It's delicious with sweet potato fries, chicken fingers, or burgers. Try it on toasted, sliced French bread. Spread a big spoonful of fermented ketchup, add chopped fresh basil leaves and drizzle with olive oil: a simple and flawless appetizer. For the perfect topping, add a small slice of ham.

Have you ever tried pineapple chutney (see page 40). Traditional chutney is made from fruits, vegetables, and / or herbs with vinegar, sugar, and spices. Fermented pineapple chutney has a wonderful flavor and all the health benefits of fermentation. Eat it with fish, chicken, or ham, or put it on yogurt – the best snack!

1.3 Fermented Foods are Medicinal.

Hippocrates, the father of medicine, claimed that "food is medicine". In traditional Chinese medicine, there is a similar saying: "food and medicine have the same origins". Food has curing effects just like medicine; medicine is the food you eat every day. Now, more and more, people are agreeing with this ancient wisdom. They understand that an important foundation of being healthy is to eat real food providing real nutrition. Fermented foods are part of this. They are well-prepared real foods and can be used as medicine.

It takes some effort to find *real* fermented vegetables and fruits in stores. To extend their shelf-life, most of them are pasteurized and / or have chemical preservatives added to them. There are no live beneficial microorganisms existing in them. Store-bought fermented foods can have the flavors from the fermentation but have lost their healing values. Therefore, homemade is the best choice because they are raw, alive, and medicinal.

In the last 10 years, many studies have confirmed that fermented foods are good for gut health. They improve weight maintenance; reduce the risk of cardiovascular disease and type 2 diabetes; improve glucose metabolism; improve lactose intolerance; and alter mood and brain activity, among other benefits.

1.3.1 Fermented Foods and the Gastrointestinal (GI) Tract

Fermented foods are a vehicle carrying a large number of micro-organisms. They contain about 10^6 to 10^9 live beneficial bacteria in every gram or milliliter. That means a very small bite of a fermented food contains a huge number of living cells. Some studies have demonstrated that a large percentage of these microbes survive the journey through the gut lumen. They increase the number of microbes by up to 10,000-fold. Consuming "living" fermented foods introduces new intestinal microbes.

Many people worry about whether these beneficial bacteria can pass through the GI tract. Actually, the fermented foods and micro-organisms do go through the whole GI tract but on the way, they experience challenges. In the mouth, they meet with enzymes and the anti-microbial constituents in the saliva; in the stomach, strong acidity, as well as the digestive enzymes, pepsin and trypsin are waiting for them; in the small intestine, they are impeded by bile salts and further enzymes. A large number of microorganisms die on the journey. However, research evidence shows that some of them survive.

Nature published a study in 2018 on changes in gut flora after eating cheese and cured meats. The scientists involved collected the stool of all participants and did RNA extraction. They found the strain of lactic acid bacteria used to make cheese and non-lactic acid bacteria used to make fermented sausage. That means these micro-organisms not only passed through the digestive system but were also metabolically active in the gut (David LA, Maurice CF, Carmody RN, et al. Diet rapidly and reproducibly alter the human gut microbiome. *Nature*. 2014,505: 559 - 563).

Another study of fermented milk in 2014 revealed similar result. Thirty-two participants with irritable bowel syndrome (IBS) were randomly assigned into two groups: a fermented milk products (FMP) group and an acidified milk product (MF) group. They consumed the fermented milk and acidified milk products twice a day. After four weeks scientists found bacteria from the fermented milk products in the stool samples of FMP group, verified through DNA extraction and sequencing. The participants in the FMP group with IBS reported that their conditions had improved, which suggested that these friendly bacteria, support gut health for patients with IBS (Veiga P, Pons P, Agrawal A, et al. Changes of the human gut microbiome induced by a fermented milk product. *Scientific Reports*. 2014, 4:6328).

1.3.2 Fermented Foods and Chronic Diseases

More and more scientific evidence has shown that eating fermented foods improves the health of people with chronic diseases. Two good-quality clinical studies on fermented foods are summarized here. *Biomed Central Medicine* (BMC Medicine) published a meta-analysis about dairy consumption and the risk of type 2 diabetes (T2D). This group of scientists used the data from three cohort studies involving 3,984,203 person-years of follow-up from 1980 to 2010. Diet was assessed by validated food frequency questionnaires, and the data were updated every four years. Incident T2D was confirmed by a validated supplement questionnaire. Their conclusion was "Higher intake of yogurt is associated with a reduced risk of T2D, whereas other dairy foods and consumption of total dairy are not associated with incidence of T2D."

Another group of scientists reviewed the health benefits of fermented foods in a study published at *ScienceDirect* in 2017. They retrieved 15 recent studies on fermented foods, focusing on improving chronic diseases including T2D, coronary heart disease, impaired glucose metabolism, obesity, cardiovascular disease, hyperlipidemia, hypertension, osteoporosis, muscle soreness, IBS, and depression in patients with T2D. They found that consuming kefir, yogurt, kimchi and fermented soy products correlated with lower T2D risk, improved insulin sensitivity, decreased insulin resistance, enhanced body weight maintenance, improved total cholesterol and low-density lipoprotein (LDL) concentrations, suppressed muscle soreness and improved bowel movements (Marco ML, Heeney D, Binda S, et al. Health benefits of fermented food: microbiota and beyond. *Current Opinion in Biotechnology*. 2017, 44:94 - 102).

1.3.3 Fermented Foods and Gastrointestinal (GI) Disorders

There are numerous studies that suggest that fermented foods can promote gut health including the incidence, duration, and severity of some gastric intestinal illness, such as:
- viral infection of the digestive tract,
- traveler's diarrhea,
- irritable bowel syndrome,
- lactose intolerance,
- intractable Pediatric diarrhea,
- pseudo-membranous colitis.

Many different strains of lactic acid bacteria and other beneficial bacteria contribute to these benefits. They produce lactic acid to maintain acidic environment in mucous membranes, which inhibits the growth of pathogenic bacteria. They also produce a large number of active substances: hydrogen peroxide and anti-bacterial, antiviral, and anti-fungal agents. These compounds prevent pathogens from attaching in the gut.

1.3.4 Fermented Foods and the Immune System

Apart from digestive problems, fermented foods also benefit human immunity. Today, more scientists believe that our digestive tract is a part of immune system, due to the fact that the digestive lumen is coated with a bacterial layer which protects us from pathogens. The bacteria provide a natural physical barrier by "producing antibiotic-like substances, anti-fungal volatile, anti-viral substances, including interferon, lizocym (lysozyme) and surfactins, that dissolve membrane viruses and bacteria; they engage the immune system to respond appropriately to the invaders." (*Gut and Psychology Syndrome*. Dr. Natasha Campbell-McBride, 2004, Mendiform Publishing).

When these beneficial bacteria in the gut are damaged by antibiotics, drugs, inappropriate diet, stress, and other factors, pathogens can attack our digestive system and cause chronic inflammation in the lumen walls. As a result, the gut wall cells do not get the right nutrients, cannot secret immunoglobulins and other regulators, and cannot take the right immune response against pathogens. The whole immune system will be out of balance or compromised. Moreover, the abnormal flora in the gut produce lots of different unknown antibodies and toxins in the body. They are absorbed through the damaged gut wall into the blood and may even enter the brain. That is called "leaky gut" (*Gut and Psychology Syndrome*. Dr. Natasha Campbell-McBride, 2004, Medinform Publishing). When these unknown antibodies and toxins accumulate, the person starts to show autoimmune disorders or behavioral disorders, such as:

- rheumatoid arthritis,
- thyroid dysfunction,
- autism,
- depression,
- addictions,
- Schizophrenia.

Adding fermented foods into our diet can deliver beneficial bacteria to the gut, help fix the damaged gut walls, and rebuild healthy gut flora.

1.4 Making Fermented Foods is Self-Sustaining.

When I was little, my family lived in a small town of north China. Winters were cold and there were not many choices for winter vegetables. Nappa cabbages, radishes and potatoes were the main staples. In fall or the beginning of winter, each family stored about 50–100kg of nappa cabbages in a root cellar for winter. Some of these cabbages were used to make *suan cai*, a kind of fermented vegetable similar to kimchi. My family had a 30-liter fermenting crock holding 8–10 big nappa cabbages with all the liquid, which was considered medium-size at that time. It took my mom a few hours to complete the whole process, washing and packing cabbages, preparing the brine, and placing a fermenting rock on the top of the cabbages. When this project was complete, it meant the family was prepared for the winter. This crock of *suan cai* lasted the whole winter and through to early spring for a small family with 2 or 3 members at that time.

The words "self-sustaining" and "sustainable" have become popular, but what do these words mean? According to Merriam-Websterdictionary.com they mean "maintaining or be able to maintain oneself or itself by independent effort". Increasing numbers of people are inspired to be self-sustaining. Fermentation is one of the oldest methods of food preservation. It keeps foods for a long period without using refrigeration and canning. People use this technique to preserve their harvest and consume during times of food shortage or harsh conditions.

Being self-sustaining has several advantages. The first one is, as mentioned above, being prepared for difficult times with confidence. The second is economic advantages. Making your own ferments is far more inexpensive than buying them. Let's take a simple example, a 2-lb organic, green cabbage costs about $2.50–$4.00 in a grocery store. I can make about 8 cups, of sauerkraut from it (a half-gallon mason jar). Store-bought organic sauerkraut costs on average $3.49–$6.49 for 16 oz, about only 2 cups. The price is a big difference.

The work including shredding, pounding, and packing takes me about 30 minutes to finish and it is the feeling of achievement that is the third advantage: personal satisfaction. I created my own sauerkraut, and also developed a positive and healthy attitude. Additionally, I do not worry about the quality of sauerkraut because I know it is the best I can have.

The fourth advantage is diversity and creativity. Every batch of sauerkraut varies in nutrition, acidity, flavor and texture due to differences in temperature, humidity, fermentation time, quality and quantity of ingredients, strains of bacteria, and a few other factors. It is a creation of a community of microorganisms in a specific ecosystem. It is also a creation of your own because you develop a friendly environment for them.

The fifth advantage is that making fermented foods is a skill. I would say that, it goes beyond a skill to a knowledge and an attitude, even an art and a science, that you can share with and teach to others: how to preserve food, how to make medicine in your kitchen, how to have a self-sufficient lifestyle, and how to be independent and practical. It is a treasure that my mom passed down to me, which you can pass on to your children too.

CHAPTER 2

HOW TO USE FERMENTATION KITS

MAKING FERMENTED FOODS needs several basic tools. Each of them are introduced in the following chapter including:
- fermentation kit containing a fermentation lid and a glass weight,
- containers,
- knife and food processor,
- pickle packer,
- bowl,
- thermometer and hygrometer (optional),
- litmus paper (optional).

2.1 Introduction to Fermentation Kits

Before I started using fermentation kits, I used a large piece of cabbage leaf to cover the shredded cabbages when I was making sauerkraut, and plastic lids to cover the wide-mouth mason jars. They worked well. But there were two problems. One was that the cabbage leaf and some of the shredded cabbage on the top turned brown because of oxidation. They floated on the top of the pickle juice and became exposed to the air and while it didn't affect the flavor and quality of the sauerkraut, they looked ugly. I had to remove the top layer of the brown part before I could eat them. Another problem was that I had to "burp" the jar; this meant loosening the plastic lids every few days in order to release the gas generated during the fermentation process. Otherwise the jars might explode, which is rare but needs to be prevented.

Above: Fermentation lid.

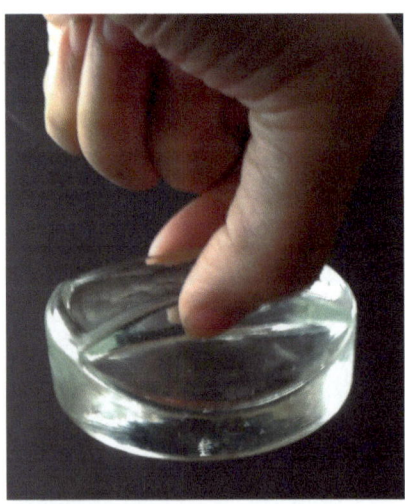

Above left and right: Fermentation weight.

Fermentation kits containing fermentation lids and glass weights, like the one pictured opposite, resolve these problems.

The plastic lids are made from 100% food-grade plastic materials and are BPA-free. The design of the lid is simple for use. The center of the lid is a tiny valve which only allows the gas, carbon dioxide, generated during the fermentation process to release. The outer layer of the valve is a month and date tracker. It is convenient for tracking the date. This size of lids can go with pint and quart sized, wide-mouth mason jars and can be used in all kinds of fermented vegetables, fruits, dairy and beverages.

There are different designs of fermenting lids on the market, such as water-sealed airlock or silicone lids. They are all good. Choose the one you like or are familiar with. I prefer this one because it is simpler, prettier, and meets all the requirements necessary for fermentation.

Glass weights keep shredded vegetables under the juice or brine, so you don't need a cabbage leaf, or a piece of rock, or a plastic bag full of water to cover them. When lactic acid bacteria start to work, the gas releases. There is no oxidation, so no brown discoloration of the vegetables. Their all around performance is very good.

The glass weights are made from 100% lime-soda glass and are very safe for storing food. They are lead-free, do not leach, and are ideal to use for making fermented vegetables. The glass weights are a modern alternative to the fermenting rocks that people used for in earlier times. This glass weight is round in shape and has a handle, so it's easy to place and lift. The diameter is 2.7 inches and weighs about 7 oz, which fits all sizes of wide-mouth mason jars. If the recipe calls for shredded vegetables, then glass weights will be very useful.

There are three main advantages to using fermentation kits which are simple, safe, and efficient. Other advantages are:
- simple operation,
- no need to burp the jars,
- no worry about explosions,
- no need to check if the water has evaporated if using water-sealed airlock,
- easy tracking of the fermentation date.

Mockingbird Bell LLC sells fermentation kits on Amazon (see page 55 for details). They are convenient for beginners or anyone who is looking to make fermentation simpler and easier.

2.2 How to Use Fermentation Kits

2.2.1 Using Glass Weights
Place the glass weight on the top of the vegetable mixture.

2.2.2 Using Fermenting Lids
After filling a wide-mouth mason jar, place the fermenting lid on the top of and twist it tightly. Set the month and date tracker.

2.3 What Else Do I Need?

2.3.1 Cleanliness
All the tools and kits you use for making fermented foods should be clean. There should be no visible dirt on the surface of the tools and work table. They should be washed, but it's not necessary to sanitize them. Your aim is to produce a friendly environment for beneficial bacteria to grow, but you don't want putrefying bacteria to compete with them. If there is mold on the surface of your tools, you need to wash and sanitize them before working.

2.3.2 Tools
1. **Wide-mouth mason jars.** Several different types of containers are available to use, such as open stoneware pots, Harsch crock pots, or glass jars. Some of them are traditional and classic. I recommend wide-mouth mason jars because they are inexpensive, lightweight, easy to source, and easy to observe.

2. **Knife and food processor.** Use for cutting and shredding vegetables or fruits.

3. **Pickle packer.** If making sauerkraut, you may need a pickle packer to pound the vegetables. The purpose of pounding is to slightly break down the cabbage cells to release the liquid inside. It usually takes 15–20 minutes to complete. Pickle packers on the market are typically made from wood. They are also called "sauerkraut pounders". If you don't have one to hand, use a potato masher or meat hammer as a substitute. For a large amount of vegetables, such as 2–3 quarts, a potato masher is more convenient. Most of the time I use a potato masher or a wooden rod (1–2 inches in diameter, 12–36 inches long) for pounding.

4. **A bowl.** A big bowl is needed to hold shredded vegetables when pounding them.

5. **Thermometer and hygrometer (optional).** Use to check temperature and humidity. If making wine, a hydrometer will be useful for measuring alcohol content.

6. **Litmus paper (optional).** Use to test pH-value.

2.3.3 Materials

1. **Vegetables and fruits.** Choose organic and fresh vegetables and fruits to make fermented products. Local farmers' markets are a good source. Some farms offer U-pick programs that mean you can harvest vegetables and fruits directly from bushes or trees. Even better is if you grow your own. Avoid using vegetables or fruits that grow too rapidly, or are over-fertilized or sprayed with pesticides. They can spoil during fermentation.

2. **Spices and herbs.** Spices are a great source of magnesium and other minerals. Fresh herbs have many health-improving qualities as well as being rich in vitamins and minerals. Most spices and herbs can be used when making fermented foods. The commonly used ones are peppercorns, dill, caraway seeds and cinnamon bark. As with vegetables and fruits, choose organically produced ones.

3. **Salt.** Unrefined sea salt with light gray color is good to use, as well as pink Himalayan salt. These contain high moisture and trace minerals. Canning salt, kosher salt and pickling salt are good to use too. Highly refined table salt should be avoided because it is chemically processed. Magnesium salts and other minerals have been removed from table salts, and aluminum, potassium iodide and dextrose have been added, which are not useful to our bodies, and can be toxic.

    Fermentation can fail if insufficient salt is used. Salt is the preservative to bridge the time until lactic acid is formed. How much salt should be added? In *The Art of Fermentation*, Sandor Katz uses a general guide, 1.5–2% weight of vegetables or roughly 1½–2 tablespoons per lb, with dry-salt method. *The Noma Guide to Fermentation* (René Redzepi & David Zilber, Artisan, 2018) recommends precise salt measurements, 2% salt to a kilogram of vegetables or fruits. Either of the two methods is fine.

    For me, I follow a simple rule learned from Sally Fallon in her book *Nourishing Traditions*. In general, I use 1 tablespoon of sea salt for a quart-size mason jar of fermented vegetables. It is easy to remember and apply, and has not failed. You can adjust it a little according to your taste.

4. **Water.** Use spring or filtered water to wash the vegetables or fruits, and to add into vegetable mixtures. The main concern when using tap water is chlorine. Chlorine is anti-microbial. If using tap water to make ferments, you may find that fermentation is delayed, or does not even start, and eventually mold starts to grow. My ferments didn't work when I used tap water. Unfortunately, a few years ago I used tap water to rinse dirt off green and red cabbages before shredding, about 20 lb of them. The final mixture did not ferment and finally turned moldy, eventually contributing to the compost pile!

   Another worry about tap water is fluoride. The chemical used to fluoridate drinking water in the U.S. is not pharmaceutical grade fluoride, but a hazardous industrial waste version of flouride. It has the potential to damage the teeth, brain, endocrine system (including the thyroid and pineal glands), bone, kidney and other tissues (*The Case Against Fluoride*. Paul Connett, James Beck, & H.S.Micklem, Chelsea Green Publishing, 2010.). Three scientists have made clear explanations about how hazardous the fluoride in tap water is. So try to avoid using tap water for making ferments.

5. **Whey.** Whey is used as the inoculant to start the fermentation process. It is the liquid separated from the curd of fermented milk such as yogurt or kefir. It contains lots of live lactic acid bacteria. Adding whey to your vegetables and fruits mixture can help start fermentation. Store-bought dry whey, however, does not have any live beneficial bacteria after the industrial process, so it cannot be used for making ferments. I prefer to use whey because it is easier to achieve successful ferments when using it, especially when making fermented fruits. Whey is simple to make at home (see Whey recipe on page 47).

6. **Other starter cultures (optional).** Juice from a previous batch of fermented products can be used as a starter culture, also called back-slopping, but this doesn't guarantee success because fermentation is a dynamic process, and the bacterial composition of the finished products is very different from that found in any previous batches. So, if you use high-quality fresh vegetables and fruits, mix the right ingredients, follow the instructions, and you should not have any problems getting started with your fermentation.

2.4 How Do I Know the Fermentation is Successful?

A successful fermentation develops a characteristic, pleasing aroma. The taste should be pleasant and slightly sour. In general, a room temperature of 70–73°F is sufficient to initiate a lacto-fermentation in about 2–4 days. They can be eaten immediately after the initial fermentation, but the flavor increases with time. You can sample them every few days to check if they are to your liking.

Another way to check if your work is successful is to use some litmus paper, which you can buy from local drugstores, to test the pH-value. For lacto-fermentation, the critical pH is 4.1. Below this pH-value, decay cannot happen.

Decomposition or decay or mold has an unpleasant smell. When it occurs, the vegetables turn slimy, and a brown, black, green, or gray layer forms on the top of the vegetables or fruits. Throw them away and start a new batch!

2.5 Storing Your Fermented Products

After 2–4 days of fermentation, the jars with the fermenting lids need to be transferred to a cool place or refrigerator. The fermentation process will massively slow down at a low temperature, but carbon dioxide still releases through the valve of the fermenting lids. The products can be kept for a long time. The taste and aroma of your products will develop with time. Sauerkraut takes about 5–6 month to fully mature. Lacto-fermented fruits such as chutney should be eaten in 2 months. For a fermented milk product such as kefir, it is better to consume it within a month because storing it for too long makes it tarter and bitter, and it loses its texture.

CHAPTER 3

RECIPES

3.1 Vegetables

Most vegetables can be used to make ferments, such as cabbages, carrots, beans, radishes, beets, cucumbers, cauliflowers, and tomatoes. Sauerkraut and kimchi are two of the popular and traditional ones. Ginger carrots and pickled radish are the best introduction for beginners. They taste great! Pickled cucumber, which is lacto-fermented, is very refreshing and less acid than pickles preserved in vinegar. Lacto-fermented ketchup is a wonderful example of a condiment that carries health benefits. Fermented salsa is another super-flavorful condiment which is easy to make in your kitchen. I also included Mom's Sichuan Pao Cai which is a traditional fermented vegetable from China.

SAUERKRAUT

Makes half gallon
1 medium cabbage, cored and shredded
1 medium red apple, cored and thinly sliced
1 tbsp caraway seeds
1 tbsp sea salt
4 tbsps whey (if not available, use an additional 1 tbsp salt)
Spring or filtered water (optional)

1. Mix the cabbage with caraway seeds, sea salt and whey in a bowl. Pound the mixture with a potato masher or meat hammer for about 10 minutes.
2. Place the mixture in a quart-sized, wide-mouth mason jar and press down firmly with the masher or meat hammer until juices come to the top of the cabbage. The top of the cabbage should be at least 1 inch below the top of the jar.
3. Use a glass weight to cover the mix, and press down so the juice covers the weight. If the juice is not enough, add some spring or filtered water to cover the top.
4. Twist the fermenting lid on the top of the jar tightly, set the date tracker, and keep at room temperature for about 3 days before transferring to cold storage.

KIMCHI

Makes 2 quarts

1 head nappa cabbage, cored and shredded
2 bunches green onions, chopped
1 cup carrots, grated
½ cup daikon radish, grated (optional)
2 tbsps freshly grated ginger
3 cloves garlic, peeled and minced
1 tsp dried chile flakes
1 tbsp sea salt
4 tbsps whey (if not available, use an additional 1 tbsp salt)

1. Place all the ingredients in a bowl and pound with a potato masher or a meat hammer to release the juices.
2. Place the mixture in a wide-mouth mason jar and press down firmly with a potato masher or a meat hammer until the juices just cover the top of the cabbage. The top of the vegetables should be at least 1 inch below the top of the jar.
3. Use a glass weight to cover the vegetables, and press down so the juice covers the weight.
4. Twist the fermenting lid on the top of jar tightly, set the date tracker, and keep at room temperature for about 3 days before transferring to cold storage.

GINGER CARROTS

Makes 1 quart
4 cups grated carrots, tightly packed
2 tbsps freshly grated ginger
1 tbsp sea salt
4 tbsps whey (if not available, use an additional 1 tbsp salt)
Spring or filtered water (optional)

This is a good recipe for beginners. It is easy to make and the taste is delicious; it goes particularly well with beef and chicken.

1. Mix all ingredients in a big bowl, and pound with a potato masher or a meat hammer to release the juices.
2. Place the mix in a mason jar and press down firmly until the juice covers the carrots. Add some spring or filtered water if there is not enough juice. The top of the carrots should be at least 1 inch below the top of the jar.
3. Place a glass weight on the top of carrots.
4. Twist the fermenting lid on the top of the jar tightly, set the date tracker, and keep at room temperature for about 3 days before transferring to a cold place or refrigerator.

PICKLED RADISH

Makes 1 quart
2 lbs red, green or daikon radish, peeled and thinly sliced
1 tbsp sea salt
4 tbsps whey (if not available, use an additional 1 tbsp salt)

Radish is popular in Oriental cuisine. This is another simple recipe and good for beginners. The flavor is mild and the texture crunchy.

1. Mix the ingredients in a big bowl and pound with a pickle packer or potato masher to release the juices.
2. Pack the mixture lightly with a pickle packer or potato masher into a wide-mouth mason jar. The top of the radishes should be at least 1 inch below the top of the jar with the juices just covering them.
3. Use a glass weight to cover the mix, and press down so the juice covers the weight.
3. Cover the jar tightly with the fermenting lid, set the date tracker, and keep at room temperature for about 3 days before transferring to cold storage.

PICKLED CUCUMBERS

Makes 1 quart
4–5 pickling cucumbers, washed
1 tbsp mustard seed
2 tbsps fresh dill, snipped
1 tbsp sea salt
4 tbsps whey (if not available, use an additional 1 tbsp of salt)
1 cup filtered water

1. Place the cucumbers in a quart-size, wide-mouth mason jar.
2. Combine the remaining ingredients and add to the jar, adding more water if necessary to cover the cucumbers. The top of the liquid should be at least 1 inch below the top of the jar.
3. Cover tightly with the fermenting lid and keep at room temperature for about 3 days before moving to a cold storage.

SALSA

Makes 1 quart

4 medium tomatoes, peeled, seeded and diced
2 small onions, finely chopped
1 cup chopped chili pepper, hot or mild
8 cloves garlic, peeled and finely chopped
1 bunch cilantro, chopped
½ tsp dried oregano
juice of 2 lemons
1 tbsp sea salt
4 tbsps whey (if not available, use an additional 1 tbsp salt)
¼ cup filtered water

1. Mix all ingredients and place in a quart-sized, wide-mouth mason jar.
2. Press down lightly with a potato masher or a meat hammer, adding more water if necessary to cover the vegetables. The top of the vegetables should be at least 1 inch below the top of the jar.
3. Cover the jar tightly with the fermenting lid, set the date tracker, and keep at room temperature for about 3 days before transferring to cold storage.

KETCHUP

Makes 1 quart
3 cups canned organic tomato paste
¼ cup whey
1 tbsp sea salt
½ cup maple syrup
¼ tsp cayenne pepper
3 cloves garlic, peeled and mashed
½ cup fish sauce

1. Mix all ingredients in a big bowl.
2. Place the mixture into a quart-sized, wide-mouth mason jar. The top of the mixture should be at least 1 inch below the top of the jar.
3. Cover the jar tightly with the fermenting lid, set the date tracker, and keep at room temperature for about 3 days before transferring to cold storage.

MOM'S SICHUAN PAO CAI

Sichuan *Pao Cai* originates from the Sichuan and Guizhou provinces located in the southwest of China. It is now popular around the world. Authentic Sichuan *Pao Cai* is sour, spicy, aromatic and crunchy. It is an essential condiment in Sichuan cuisine. The commonly used vegetables are cabbage, radish, green or asparagus beans, carrots, hot chili peppers, garlic, and ginger. The brine method is the way to make Sichuan *Pao Cai*. Some recipes are complicated. They call for cane sugar, rice porridge, greater than 40% (or 80 proof) grain alcohol or vodka. My mom has been using the following recipe for many years without failure. It is a simple and practical one. No sugar or white liquor is required. The most important thing is cleanliness. Hands, vegetables, and tools including pots, knife, cutting board, chopsticks or tongs should be dry and clean without any water and oil. The jar, fermenting lids, and glass weight should be sterile. This guarantees a successful batch of Sichuan *Pao Cai*.

Makes 1 quart

3 cups filtered or spring water
1 tsp red (or Sichuan) peppercorns
½ lb green or red cabbage, rinsed in spring or filtered water, air dried and cut into big bite sizes
¼ lb daikon or radish, rinsed in spring or filtered water, air dried and thinly sliced
¼ lb carrots, rinsed in spring or filtered water, air dried, peeled and thinly cut diagonal
2–3 whole green or red chili peppers
1 head of garlic, peeled
6 fresh peeled and sliced ginger
2 tbsps kosher salt

1. First make the brine. Bring water and the peppercorns to a boil in a saucepan and removed from the heat. Let it cool to room temperature.
2. Place all the prepared vegetables in a wide-mouth mason jar. The top of the vegetables should be 2 inches below the top of the jar.
3. Add the salt to the vegetables.
4. Place the glass weight on the top.
5. Add the brine to the jar until it covers the top of the glass weight. Place the fermenting lid on the top of the jar and twist it tightly. Set the date tracker.
6. Sit the jar in a cool, dark place. Sample the vegetables every one or two days to check if the sourness is to your liking. It should be ready to eat in 1–2 weeks.

3.2 Fruits

Chutney is a mixture of fruits and / or vegetables and spices. Lacto-fermented pineapple chutney is easy to make, colorful, and full of enzymes, vitamins, and probiotics. Apricot butter is sweet and versatile. It can be paired with cheese, or spread for breakfast, or a snack.

PINEAPPLE CHUTNEY

Makes 1 quart
1 small pineapple, peeled and cut into small cubes
1 bunch cilantro, coarsely chopped
2 tbsps freshly grated ginger
2 tbsps fresh lime juice
1 tsp sea salt
¼ cup whey
½ cup filtered water

1. Mix the pineapple, cilantro and ginger and place in a quart-sized, wide-mouth mason jar.
2. Press down lightly with a potato masher or a meat hammer.
3. Mix the lime juice, sea salt and whey with water and pour over the pineapple, adding more water if necessary to cover the pineapple. The mixture should be at least 1 inch below the top of the jar.
4. Place a glass weight on the top of the mixture.
5. Twist the fermenting lid on the top of the jar tightly and set the date tracker. Leave at room temperature for about 2 days before transferring to the refrigerator. This should be eaten within 2 months.

APRICOT BUTTER

Makes 2 quarts
4 cups unsulphured dried apricots
Spring or filtered water
1½ tbsp sea salt
¼ cup whey
¼ cup raw honey

This is excellent with breakfast porridge or on pancakes.

1. Place the apricots in a saucepan and add water to cover them. Bring to the boil and cook on a medium to low heat for a few minutes. Remove the saucepan from the heat and cool. The apricot will absorb the water and turn soft. Transfer with a slotted spoon to a food processor.
2. Process with the remaining ingredients. Taste for sweetness and add more honey if necessary.
3. Place the mixture in quart-sized, wide-mouth mason jars. The apricot butter should be at least 1 inch below the top if the jars.
4. Place the fermenting lid on the top of the jar and twist it tightly. Set the date tracker, and keep at room temperature for about 2 days before transferring to the refrigerator. This should be eaten within 2 months.

3.3 Beverages

Homemade beverages are unique substitutes for commercial ones. They avoid caffeine, large amount of sugar and alcohol, and are enhanced by the fermentation process. Their nutrients are more available, and they supply the gastrointestinal tract with beneficial bacteria. Ginger ale is a refreshing pick-me-up and a digestive aid. It especially relieves thirst after physical activities. Beet kvass is valued for its medicinal property. It is super for fasting and detoxification.

GINGER ALE

Makes 2 quarts
¾ cup ginger, peeled and finely chopped or grated
½ cup fresh lime juice
¼–½ cup coconut sugar or raw cane sugar
2 teaspoons sea salt
¼ cup whey
2 quarts filtered water

1. Place all the ingredients in two quart-size mason jars. Stir well and cover with the fermenting lid tightly.
2. Leave at room temperature for 2–3 days before transferring to the refrigerator. It will keep several months well chilled.
3. To serve, strain into a glass.

BEET KVASS

Makes 2 quarts
3 medium or 2 large organic beets, peeled and chopped up coarsely
¼ cup whey
1 tablespoon sea salt
filtered water

This drink is valuable for its medicinal qualities and as a digestive aid. Drinking one 4 oz glass of beet kvass in the morning and night is an excellent blood tonic, improves regularity, aids digestion, alkalizes the blood, and cleanses the liver. It is a good treatment for kidney stones and other ailments (*Nourishing Traditions*. Sally Fallon, New Trend Publishing, 2001).

1. Place the beets, whey and salt in a quart-size mason jar. Add water to fill the container. Stir well and cover with the fermenting lid tightly.
2. Leave at room temperature for 2–3 days before transferring to the refrigerator.
3. When most of liquid has been drunk, refill the jar with filtered water and keep at room temperature another 2 days. The resulting brew will be slightly less strong than the first. After the second brew, throw away the beets and start again.

3.4 Dairy

Fermented dairy products play an important role in many traditional cuisines. Lactic acid bacteria break down milk sugar (lactose) and milk protein (casein) to make it a more assimilable for people. Kefir is a microbial-rich food that helps improve the inner ecology. It is a drink-style yogurt from cow, goat or sheep's milk. It tastes a little tart and contains different microorganisms to yogurt. Whey has many uses in the kitchen. It is yellowish liquid that separates from yogurt, kefir, or other cultured dairy products. It is rich in vitamin B2, amino acid, and potassium. It helps digestion and detoxification. It can be used to make lemonade and smoothies, soak grains, or drink straight. We use it as a starter culture or an inoculant for fermented vegetables, fruits, or beverages.

KEFIR

Makes 2 cups
2 cups fresh cow or goat raw milk
1 tbsp kefir grains or 1 package kefir powder
  or 4 tbsps of kefir from a previous batch

Kefir is very easy to make at home. The version made from kefir grain tastes stronger than the version made from kefir powder.

1. If using kefir grains, put them in a fine strainer and rinse them with filtered water. Place the milk in a quart-size, wide-mouth mason jar.
2. Add the kefir grains, or powder, or kefir from a previous batch, to the milk and stir well. Put on the fermenting lid and leave at room temperature for 12 hours to 2 days.
3. Stir and taste the kefir every 12 hours. When it reaches the tartness to your liking, the kefir is ready. Then move to the refrigerator. It's best to consume it within 1 month.

WHEY

Makes 5 cups whey (and 2 cups cream cheese)
2 quarts yogurt, kefir, or raw milk

Whey is widely used as an inoculant for making lacto-fermented vegetables and fruits. Cream cheese is a by-product during the creation of whey. If using yogurt or kefir, choose a good-quality commercial plain one or homemade. If using raw milk, allow the milk to stand in a clean glass container at room temperature for 2–4 days until it separates.

1. Set a large strainer over a bowl and line it with a clean cheesecloth. Pour in the yogurt or separated milk, and let it stand for several minutes to allow the whey to run into the bowl.
2. Tie up the cheesecloth with the milk solids inside. Tie the little sack to a wooden spoon placed across the top of a container so that more whey can drip out.
3. When the dripping stops, the cheese is ready. It takes 4–6 hours. Store the whey in a mason jar and the cheese in a glass container. Whey can be kept for about 6 months and cheese for 1 month in the refrigerator.

3.5 Grain

There is a long history of people using fermented grains to make their foods, such as sourdough bread, beer, and sake. After fermentation, the phytic acid in grains, which may be the trigger of gluten sensitivity for some people, is neutralized. In addition, vitamins and proteins locked in the grain become more bioavailable through the fermentation process.

JIU NIANG (SWEET RICE WINE)

Jiu Niang is a traditional Chinese food, also called sweet rice wine or *Jiu Zao*. It is sweet and aromatic. Though it is called wine, the alcohol content is very low. In China, *Jiu Niang* is widely used as a dessert or snack. In addition, it is nutritious and easy to digest. Jiu Niang is also popular for postpartum women to improve energy and milk production.

Making *Jiu Niang* at home is very easy. Sweet rice and yeast balls are available in most Asian food markets or online. Sweet rice is also called glutinous rice or sticky rice. The yeast ball is a mix of mold, yeast and bacteria. It takes these microorganisms about 24 hours to work at 80–85°F. I usually put the prepared batch into the oven with the light on for incubation.

Makes 1 pint
1 cup sweet rice
1 cup spring or filtered water
1 tbsp yeast ball, crushed

1. Place the rice in a medium-size bowl which fits in the steamer. Rinse the rice 2–3 times and soak in 1 cup of water overnight. The rice will absorb the water and the volume will expand.
2. Put the bowl with the rice and some remained water in the steamer and steam for 30 minutes till the rice turns transparent. If you use a rice cooker, follow the manufacturer's instructions to cook the sweet rice.
3. Remove the cooked rice from the heat and stir to loosen. Let it cool at room temperature.
4. Use clean hands or a spoon to mix the crushed yeast powder with the cool rice.
5. Pack the mixture in a wide-mouth mason jar. Place the fermentation lid on the top of the jar and twist it tightly.
6. Place the jar in a warm place 80–85°F for 24 hours. Move to refrigerator when it is done.

3.6 Making Wine from Fruits

People have been fermenting fruit juices for thousands of years. In fact, fermentation of fruit juice cannot be prevented, unless the juice is pasteurized or refrigerated. The production of fermented beverages has been an important way to preserve fruit throughout history. There are many books on the subject and there are many different ways of doing it. Fine wines are produced using very specific methods. A huge variety in the types and flavors of beer are produced by using different fermentation methods. You could spend a lifetime mastering all the fine details related to the creations of fine wines and beers. But there are very simple ways to make wine. Fermenting fruit juice is not difficult; before refrigerators, our ancestors did it as part of everyday life. And anyway, who has time for complicated work? This recipe shows you the simplest and quickest way to make delicious fermented fruit juices.

Fermentation occurs when yeast transforms the sugar present in fruit juice into alcohol (ethanol) and carbon dioxide. Unless fruit is treated to kill them, natural yeasts are present in fruit when it is harvested. This appears as the "bloom" or "blush" on the skin of grapes. It looks like a little bit of white dust. There are many different kinds of wild yeasts. For high-quality products, like wine, the natural yeasts are replaced by cultured yeasts before fermentation starts. The use of cultured yeasts produces consistent results and flavor (or perhaps, more accurately, more consistent results). But good results, if somewhat unpredictable, are possible using the wild yeast present on the fruit when it is harvested. That is what I will show here.

3.6.1 No Fuss Wine

Before starting, prepare your utensils and tools. They should be clean. Wash them as you would your dishes, they don't need to be sterile. You will need the following items:
- containers to hold fruit,
- containers to hold fruit juice,
- funnels,
- fermentation vessel,
- fermentation lock,
- siphon hose,
- large spoons or scrapers.

The first step in producing fermented fruit juice is to get some fruit. Any kind of fruit can be fermented. Grapes and apples are the most commonly used fruits. Pears and various berries are easily used as well. Sugar water can be fermented,

which is what mead is, fermented honey in water, but in these cases cultured yeast needs to be added to the batch. The fruit you get should be as natural as you can find.

Much of the commercially produced fruit in the grocery store has been treated with preservatives and insecticides. These can inhibit fermentation and force the use of cultured yeast. Organically grown fruit straight from the tree, vine or bush is the best material to use. The "pretty" fruit found in the grocery store is not necessary. Blemished fruit works just fine.

If the fruit is straight from the tree, bush or vine, it doesn't need to be washed prior to use. If there is dirt that needs to be removed, don't use chlorine containing tap water. The chlorine can kill the naturally present yeast. Chlorine can be removed from tap water purified by reverse osmosis or with a carbon filter. Bottled spring water from the grocery store can be used for rinsing the fruit.

The first step in processing fruit for fermentation is to crush or grind it. For processing a few gallons of juice, a food processor or blender works satisfactorily. For larger volumes a meat grinder works well. There are purpose made fruit grinders and commercial scale equipment. These are readily found with an internet search. If using a small meat grinder, the fruit must be cut up so that it will fit into the throat of the grinder. For example, apples need to be quartered. This is a lot of work. A large meat grinder with a 4-inch opening is the most convenient way to grind large volumes of fruit without having to first cut it up. (These are hard to find and cost almost $1,000.)

The next step is to press the juice out of the ground fruit pulp. For projects of a few gallons, a clean dish cloth or piece of cheesecloth can be used. Put some pulp in the cloth and twist it to squeeze out the juice. For larger volumes of pulp use a fruit press. There are several different types from different suppliers. Pressing is heavy work, so it is important to get a heavy duty press. A five gallon capacity press is convenient to use. Put the ground fruit pulp into the press and squeeze out the juice. The pump should be almost dry when the pressing is done, it will be damp to the touch.

This is where simplification is possible. Some people filter the juice to removed particulate matter. Some people do a two-step fermentation where the particulate matter is removed after a few days by decanting. A simpler method is to just put the particulate laden juice in the fermentation vessel and let the fermation process run. When the process is done, the sediment can be removed by decanting. Glass or stainless steel fermentation vessels are preferred. A 5-gallon glass carboy (a big bottle) is convenient to use. Food grade plastic and Teflon vessels are used, but any plastic container will permit a small amount of the plastic to dissolve (called plasticizer) into the wine. It is a matter of personal choice about how much plasticizer you want to ingest.

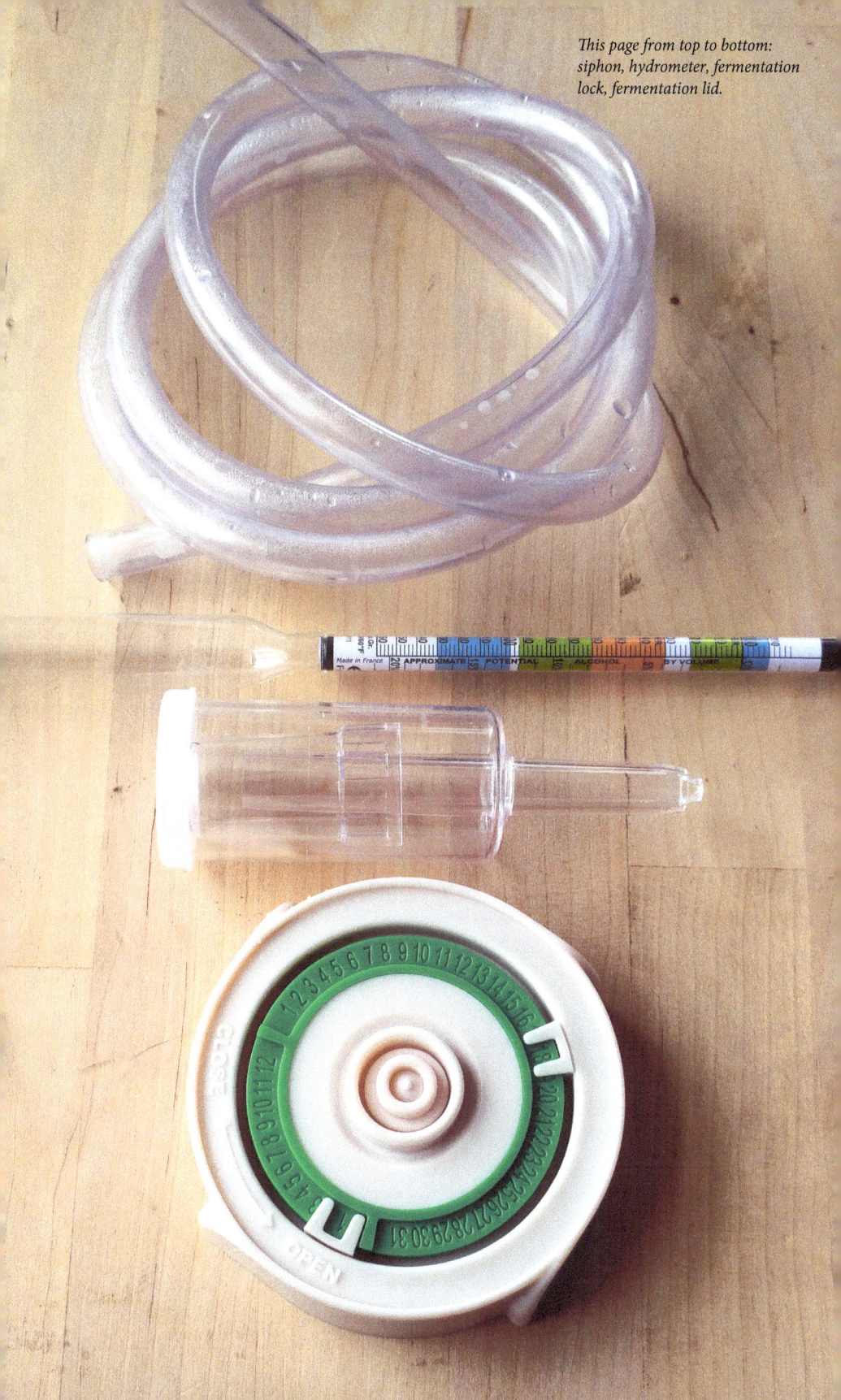

This page from top to bottom: siphon, hydrometer, fermentation lock, fermentation lid.

When the fermenting vessel is full, leave a little air space at the top and put a fermentation lock on the vessel. When the fermentation process gets going, it bubbles a lot. If there is too little space at the top, the fluid in the vessel will bubble out, through the fermentation lock, creating a mess.

A fermentation lock is a device that isolates the air inside the fermentation vessel from the room air. Fermentation is an anaerobic process. That means that no oxygen from the air can be permitted to contact the fermenting materials. If oxygen from the air gets into the fermentation vessel, the batch will be ruined. The carbon dioxide produced by fermentation is heavier than the oxygen and nitrogen in air. As the carbon dioxide is produced, the nitrogen and oxygen float on top of the carbon dioxide and are forced out of the lock.

There are two types of fermentation locks. One is a looped glass or plastic tube that holds a little water. The water blocks air from getting into the fermentation vessel, but lets the carbon dioxide formed during the fermenting escape. A second type of lock is the fermenting lids which use a rubber gasket to seal out the air. When pressure builds up, the flap lifts a little, letting the gas out. This type fits mason jars and is good for fermenting small volumes.

The natural yeast present in the fruit will be sufficient to get the fermentation process going. Let the vessel sit at room temperature to ferment. Fermenting can occur at a temperature as low as 45°F. The fermentation temperature can go up to 85°F. The rate of fermentation increases with increasing temperature. The desired rate of fermentation varies according to the type of wine being made. For general purposes, a temperature range of 65–75°F will work satisfactorily. Do keep in mind that the fermentation generates heat, so if many fermentation vessels are in a small room, the room temperature could rise above the desired range. If the fermentation vessel gets too cool, fermentation will stop. It will resume again with no problem, when the vessel gets warm enough. However, if the vessel gets too hot, the wine can be damaged.

The fermentation will continue for a few weeks to a month or so. While fermentation is in process make sure the room temperature is stable. Ensure that the water in the fermentation lock does not evaporate if using it. Add more (not chlorinated tap water) if necessary. If using a fermenting lid, there is no water to worry about.

When the fermentation process is completed, decant the wine from the container into bottles. Use of a siphon makes this easier. You can put the wine into wine bottles and cork it. Bottles, corks and a corking jig can be obtained from a wine making store. Or you can just put it in mason jars and keep it in the refrigerator.

If you put the wine into corked bottles, make sure the fermentation is complete. If not, fermentation will continue and produce more carbon dioxide. If the amount of carbon dioxide is small, you will get sparkling wine. If it too much, the bottle will explode.

If you want to measure the alcohol content of your wine, you will need a hydrometer to measure the specific gravity of the wine. Measure the specific gravity of the fruit juice before you start fermenting. Measure it again when fermentation is complete. Use this equation to calculate the alcohol content:

$$\%ABV = \left(\frac{Original\ SG - Final\ SG}{7.36}\right) \times 1,000$$

%ABV means percentage alcohol by volume;
SG means specific gravity.

Here is an example of the calculation. If the specific gravity of the batch was 1.06 and after fermentation it was 1.01, then the alcohol content was 6.8%.

$$\%ABV = \left(\frac{1.06 - 1.01}{7.36}\right) \times 1,000 = 6.8\%$$

The wine produced by this process will probably be cloudy. If you let it sit for a while, the particulate matter will sink the bottom. However, the presence of the cloudy material doesn't have a noticeable effect on the flavor of the wine.

When using this method, you may occasionally have a failure, or make vinegar (which is useful as well). However, it is much less work than other methods.

Good luck with your fermentation project.

Making fermented food is both an art and a science. It looks difficult but it is easy. It is a journey to learn about the world of culture and real food, of being self-sustaining, and a part of self-healing when needed. Fermentation kits are convenient and easy to use. They help your foods develop natural and unique flavors and enhance the probiotics for your body.

The Mockingbird Bell Fermentation Kits featured in this book are available for purchase online at: https://www.amazon.com/dp/B07RS16GRB?ref=myi_title_dp and https://www.amazon.com/dp/B07RW4GGF1?ref=myi_title_dp. I hope you enjoy using them for your fermentation project!

Acknowledgements

Thank you to, my mom, for sharing your secret Sichuan *Pao Cai* recipe with me, and everything you taught me in the past.

Thanks to my family, Terry, Elizabeth, Anna, and Nancy for supporting me to complete this book.

A big thank you to the incredibly talented Paul Palmer-Edwards, who was able to make a creative cover design for this book, and who can make anything a beautiful work of art.

Thank you Sophie Elletson for your editing and meticulous patience.

Copyright © Yi Zhang
All rights reserved
ISBN: 9781733884419

www.ingramcontent.com/pod-product-compliance
Lightning Source LLC
Chambersburg PA
CBHW041821040426
42453CB00005B/126